WENDELL ETERNAL

Volume II

ORDER OF THE HIDDEN

"If you take your child to a battlefield, do not cry out to god when that child dies."

THE SUCCESSFUL BUSINESS MAN

The lights are off, but someone is home. The town veterinarian, Timmy S, is up scheming. Doc was not his preferred nickname, that's just what everyone called him. Doc had gotten tired of trying to correct people. Plus, his wife and daughter didn't think Timmy S. was cool at all. They thought it was stupid. Little did they know, Doc was a successful businessman masquerading as a town vet. Sure, he had graduated college and was a legal vet but that was not his heart's desire. Doc wanted to help animals. Once he realized euthanasia was forty-two percent of his practice, his heart changed from good to diabolical.

Ninety-four percent of the time, Docs' Day started off basically the same. He would wake up to a quiet house. Once Docs feet hit the wood floor in his bedroom, all hell would break lose. Teazer, his blue nose Pitbull, would make a mad dash to his harness. The harness was located 6 feet in the air on a small shelf. Teazer would sit under that shelf with the meanest, most intimidating look a dog could muster. This perfectly trained masterpiece of a dog would patiently set still just like a statue. Teazer, waiting on the leader of the pack, would watch the steps like a hawk. When Doc got to the bottom of the steps, the two old friends would just look intently at each other. Until Doc spoke.

 "What's up Teazer, you want to go for a run?" "BARK, BARK!" Teazer would bark Hell Yeah! Then he would jump up and grab his harness. After he grabbed his harness, he would sling it over to Doc. Then, Teazer would pat his feet and wag his tail. Walking his dog everyday not only strengthened their bond but had increased Teazers intelligence. This was no ordinary walk in the park. Doc was in damn good shape. This was no walk; this was a race. Doc slipped the harness on Teazer and then snapped on the 10-foot leash. The two adversaries headed to the back yard towards the alley. Teazer did not pull Doc, he walked calmly beside him. The two sprinters got to the alley, and it was Time!

Doc was fast, super-fast. The two took off! Rocks flying everywhere. The first 20 yards, Teazer always played possum. By the time they got to 40 yards, Teazer was smoking Doc. When Teazer began to pull Doc, he always released the leash. Teazer would then kick into another gear and leave his adversary in the dust. Teazer was so far ahead of Doc, he could barely see him. Then out of the corner of his eye, Doc saw something beside him. Doc slowed a bit and looked to his left. Judge, the massive lab-rottweiler mix, was chasing him. Doc was already gassed. He had been running full speed for over 100 yards. Judge caught up to him, barked, then lunged at Doc. Doc let out a scream and jumped straight up into the air. By the time he landed, Teazer pulled up, and he was Pissed!

This two-hundred-pound monster was getting his ass handed to him. Teazer, this 79-pound pit, had Moor game in him than a PS6. It was like watching a puma fight a tiger. Only the puma was just as strong and a lot faster. Teazer forced Judge back into his own yard. If judge had been any smaller,

he would have already been dead. Doc screamed
at Teazer, "Stop boy! Stop! Come on, lets go
home." When this didn't work, the only thing Doc
could think of was to sprint towards his house and
say, "Bye Teazer!" Teazer finally let up. He barked
a couple of times as if to say, "Your Lucky pal."
Then he followed Doc home.

THE SUCCESSFUL BUSINESS MAN Goes Vegan

  Part one of Docs two-fold plan had come to
fruition. The town vet was now the proud owner
of the only buffet restaurant in town. Not just any
restaurant. The newly renamed "Almost Vegan
Buffet." "One of a kind menu", was Doc's motto.
The only meat on the menu was chicken.
Everything else was exotic fruits and veggies from
all over the world. The special of the day never
changed but the town loved it. With the purchase
of an adult meal, children 13 and under had free

access to the giant salad bar. Basically, all the fruits and vegetables they could eat. The chicken was kept on the other side of the restaurant and had an attendant. If you were 17 and under, you had to be accompanied by an adult. It was a risk hiring the attendant, but it had paid off. The profits increased 20 percent once the attendant started checking for ids.

Part two of Docs ultimate plan was proving to be a bit Moor difficult. The town vet had already switched over to vegan soon as the buffet opened. Most people thought this was a gimmick. Doc ran radio ads saying, "The Mega Salad Bar Made Me Do "it!" When people asked him what's "it"? Doc would say, "Go Vegan!" Doc had his own reasons for going vegan and it was not a gimmick. He wanted his wife and daughter to go vegan too. Doc had explained to his wife, "Honey, come on, you've got to see the profit in this?" To which she replied, "I had an exciting and fulfilling career. I took a desk job to help you run this restaurant. Now you want to tell me it was all to get me to go vegan? Please be very careful how you answer this dear." Timmy S. had seen that look in her eyes before. The Doc knew his wife could get active if she was pissed off. People didn't last long if they got on her bad side.

"Ok, new approach," the Doc thought to himself. "That was a dead end. I'm just going to have to go facts on her." Mery loved her facts. The same way his wife could intimidate him with her icy cold stare, he could do with facts. Mery couldn't help herself when presented with cold hard facts. That's what made their bond so strong. Doc would never argue with her. If it was important enough, he would merely present her with facts. This was a lovely game of cat and mouse they both enjoyed. The Docs job was to get as many facts as possible into his wife before she caught on to what he was doing. If she caught on right away, he would lose, and she would not be interested in playing, "The Game." He would have to wait a couple of weeks.

"Hey Mery, did you hear about that restaurant that's been closed for two years? Its on the other side of town." "No Honey, what about it?" "It's for sale. The owners have been caught up in court and lawsuits for the past three years. I'm thinking a second "Almost Vegan", would put us on the map. You know, like a tourist attraction." "So, who is going to run this, Tim? You're pissing me OFF! I did not sign up for this Sh*t!" "That's the beauty. With a second location we can both retire. I've crunched the numbers." Doc slid over a folder to his wife. "FACTS!" That's the word that went through Doc's head as he passed Mery the folder. Her beloved facts. These numbers were not fudged in any way. Thus, making that folder he just slid her, "Facts!"

Mery's eyes lit up. Doc was thinking to himself. "That's it, that's it, just a little bit more." The game was unfolding, this was the moment he had been waiting for. If Mery asked him a question about the numbers, then she would be interested. While she was interested, he could then hit her with moor facts. Like the real hidden fact, he wanted to share with her. Mery continued to read as a slight smile started to crack in the corner of her mouth. Mery thought to herself. "Ok, he's got me. He took the time to prepare all this just so I could ask him a question. After I ask my question, he's going to tell me what he really wants to say. I could easily win right now. Just throw the paper aside and walk off. But I do want to get out of this damn restaurant business. "

Mery read another page and a half. Then she finally gave in. She could see that Doc had spent a lot of time on this report. Plus, Mery had a question to ask, and she wanted an immediate answer. "Ok Tim, you win. I see you drew up this fancy report with all this detail. So, I'm assuming you left the time frame and start date off intentionally." Doc replied, "I did." "Ok Tim, if I let you buy your restaurant how long will it be before we can retire?" "Assuming we get her up and running in 6 months; I would say about 18 months after that. So, lets say 2 to 3 years max."

This made Mery excited. She was super stoaked! She was hoping and praying that her husband would say 5 years or less. He had said two to three years. She was having a hard time controlling herself. If she acted too happy, Doc would never let her hear the end of it. Mery said, "I guess that could work." "Girl Stop!" Doc was laughing hard now. He knew he had won. His wives' words had come out one way, but her face told a different story. When Mery said, "I guess that will work", she had bitten down on her bottom lip and looked a way." Even with her head turned, Doc could see her smiling. "Mery, turn around and look at me. I want to see if you're happy." She couldn't take it anymore. Mery burst out laughing. "Damn "it" Tim! I'm mad at you. You got me. Ok, you win. What the hell is it that you want?"

 This was Tim's chance. He could not rush it. He had to slide smoothly. "Oh, nothing. Do you want to go there and see it? Babe it's in great shape." Mery looked at her husband with a quizzical look. She was confused. She hadn't counted on that. Mery thought to herself, "Just what the hell is he up to?" "Sure Hun, when do you want to go?" Doc knew his wife inside and out. He studied her. He knew what all her facial expression meant. Doc had seen that look on her face before. He had her. She really didn't know what the hell he was up to. My time is NOW! He answered his wife, "We can probably go tomorrow morning. We got a steal on this place Mery. The owners are losing their asses in court. Want to know what they are charged with?" "What?" "Well, it seems they got caught with a whole bunch of small tools used for preparing cats and dogs. Just, what in the hell is this world coming too? I'm glad I'm vegan." Merys mouth dropped open. Her gum fell out of her mouth. That was her and her daughter's favorite restaurant before it got shut down.

 Now, Merys face was bright purple. She was very angry. She was not mad at her husband; she was mad at herself. He had totally duped her. This was his intent the whole time. Mery thought to herself, "He did all of this, just to get us to go vegan." He had presented her with the facts, the cold hard facts. Now Mery knew her, and her daughter had been eating cat and dog three years ago when Tommy's was open. Now Doc swung the hammer and pushed the final nail into her stance on meat. He didn't need facts now. He had touched her heart. So, he continued to go the emotional route. Doc said, "Hey babe, could you imagine if someone had stolen Teazer as a pup and…….." "Just stop. Ok, Ok, I get the point. Vegan we are."

THE SUCCESSFUL BUSINESS MAN, JOB WELL DONE

Twenty-four months later Timmy S. was feeling good. No one called him Doc anymore. The "Almost Vegan II" had been wildly successful. The town vet wasn't a vet anymore. He was a successful businessman to the fullest extent. Doc was hardly ever at his office anymore. He hired another vet to do the heavy lifting for him. Doc would just over see the euthanasia and safe disposals.

The Doc wasn't having second thoughts, he just hated the waste. He thought to himself how hard he had worked to get here. Now, he was just going to give it away. The sell was final, money had already changed hands. Doc thought to himself, "I really did "it". I fooled them all."

Mery had already purchased tickets to the Swiss Alps and updated their passports. The "Town Vet" inside him had died. The Malcolm "By any Means necessary" route, had worked. This new man, Timmy S., had taken his shot and hit. Not only had he hit once, but he had also hit twice. Timmy S.

thought to himself, 'Yeah, it's time. Cash out and dip. Plus, the wife would get me killed if I even asked her about another business endeavor."

Their plane was departing Saturday. This would be the last night the trio would spend at the restaurant. Doc's daughter was sad. She loved the place. Mery was ecstatic, ready to travel the world again. Just one quick little meeting with Skimp and he was out. Skimp was Docs inside man. His scammer. Skimp handled all the food processing info. The companies that provided the products and the payments. Doc had a going away present for Skimp. Skimp had originally been pissed that his easy mill ticket was ending. Doc would give him 100 racks to smooth things over. Skimp asked to meet Doc at the restaurant. Skimp had a surprise for the doc too.

Skimp walked in with the Sheriff. He looked around, spotted Timmy S. and waved. The Doc did not wave back. A dozen moor men shot into the restaurant. THE GIG WAS UP! Skimp had got caught with meth two weeks ago and decided that he would not take his 10, he would just tell on a friend. Instead of taking ten years for the meth he got caught with; he snitched on the doctor.

Mery was amazingly calm. Normally she would have flashed her high security badge by now. Instead, she just patiently watched, trying to see why Tim was looking so dumbfounded.

Instead of properly disposing of the animals he euthanized, The Doc had been mixing it with his chicken. It had been easy. The only meat he served was chicken. Their number one bestselling item was a mix of dog, cat and chicken. The Sheriff walked up to Doc. Mery came and stood right beside him. The Sheriff spoke. "Dr. Timothy Swim, turn around and place your hands behind your back." The Sheriff began to read off Dr. Swims charges and Mery didn't even bat an eye. She was no longer Mery. That cold steal stare had returned. She was Agent Mermaid Swim.

The Sheriff cuffed the successful businessman and began to lead him to the car personally. He had a few choice words for his long-time friend. "Doc, how could you? You've scared my daughter and the rest of this town's children for life. My little Maggie loves those damn Pup Nuggets. She is going to still be asking for them. Then when she finds out…." Dr. Swim cut the Sheriff off. "I never gave them anything. It was you and her mother who showed id to get to those Pup Nuggets. So, all I can say Sheriff is, Job Well Done!"

BRACKISH WATER, WALKING LIZARD

"Folks, you don't want to miss this! The 11th annual Lizard Water Walking Races! We've got the best Basilisk lizards in the known Universe. Now folks, last year's top price took home twenty-five thousand dollars. This is a three-day event. The final race will be one hundred dollars a ticket. We support our military and……" Matt changed the channel. "Damn ads!" "Matty, are we almost there yet?" "Are we almost there yet? I told you to stop calling me Matty. It's not funny anymore. Now, it's just annoying." "Maybe I wouldn't call you Matty if you took us on a real vacation." "Trish, this is a real vacation, I'm paying real money for "it"." No Matty, I don't want to see lizard's race. Three days of you drunk watching lizards walk on water, fun meter is 0!" "Will first off, this is a gambling venture. And secondly…."

It was too late. Trish had already put her earphones in and let her seat back. She was going to be in a bitchy mood this weekend and he deserved it. Matt thought to himself, "Why did I buy ten 100 -dollar tickets? When Trish finds out I'm dead meat. Unless....one of them hits!"

The water was perfectly still and calm. Lake StarWess was the perfect setting for the race. Camp StarWess was a huge attraction for one weekend out of the year. People from all over the state came to see the water walking lizard's race. It was like a spring break festival but only for gamblers and hunters. The oddest arrangement and assortment of people that you could imagine. Add alcohol and gambling and you've got a volatile and fun environment.

The sweat heart water picnic was on Friday night and the races would start Saturday at first sun light. "Babe, do you want to go to the sweat heart water picnic tonight?" Trish thought to herself, "God why? Could this possibly get any worse?" Then she replied, "What happed to your hound staking the rabbit thing you wanted to go to?" "Trish, why do you have to be so cynical? It's called

"Hound Rabbit Stakes" it's a race." "Because it sounds like cruelty to animals Matty. And if you're cruel to the animals, the animals will be cruel to you!" Matt wasn't listening. He was thinking about his tickets for the race on Sunday. "So, ma, you wanna go or not?" "Yes, Mathew Adam the III, I will go got damn it! Just stop me by the liquor store first!" Trish did not want to go to a water picnic at night with a bunch of hunters all around the lake. The whole thing seemed dumb to her. The only thought she had running through her mind was, "I can't stand his Ass!"

Welp, she was right. This had been the worse night of her life. Literally! Bugs biting, make up running and Matt drunk. Matt had pulled a fast one on her. He told her he would go in and get her drinks. Matt got her some wine coolers and himself 10 miniatures of fireball. By the time Trish realized he was drunk, he only had three bottles left. "I'm ready to go back to the room MATT!" Matt burst out laughing and almost fell off the boat. "Oh, but wait, what happened to Matty?" Matt burst out laughing again.

Lake StarWess was huge. Trish and Matt were a 45-minute boat ride back to the boat doc. The less secluded side, they now found themselves on, had a floating store. Matt got a 12 pack of beer and some smokes. He stopped before getting back on the boat. "Damn girl, you are fine as f^ck." Trish fake smiled and then flipped him off. 'Well, what the heck was dat for?" "You're drunk Matt!" 'I'm not drunk Trishy! I'm crashing. I got beer to level me out. I could see if I had got more liquor. Damn Debbie Downer."

Three hours later, Trish was fast asleep, and Matt was even more drunk. The lake was a lot bigger than he thought. All the boat ramps looked the same in the dark. The pontoon was getting harder to navigate. Matt steered towards a huge log that was halfway in the water. He dropped anchor and could tell he was only in four to five feet of water. Matt peed on the log and started collecting all his beer bottles. After he gathered the beer bottles, he tried to toss them on the other side of the log. But he missed!

Instead, the bottles had smashed violently onto the log. "Why you little mother f^cker!" Matt was terrified. The voice he heard sounded like the boogey man. He was wondering if he had rifles aimed at him for littering. The folks in Camp StarWess were dead serious about littering. Matt timidly replied, "Whose there, what's going on? "SPLASH!" Matt didn't hear the splash, he felt it! A giant tail had smacked him across his chest and knocked him into the water. Trish woke up just in time to see the log move. Only, this was not a log. This was a massive saltwater crocodile.

Another big splash. Trish screamed! She called out to Matt. "Matt, Matt!" Then she spotted him. Trish felt so relieved. He looked hurt but at least he was alive. "Matt, get over here, come on!" Matt did not move or reply. Trish had mascara in her eyes, she could not see clearly. She cleared her eyes and squinted in the pitch-black dark of the lake water. Trish grabbed the light and flashed it on Matt. What she saw would haunt her for the rest of her life. Matt had been bitten clean in half from the waist up. His belt buckle reflected light back at Trish. Matts feet were still twitching. Trish began to scream again.

BRACKISH WATER, ALLIGATOR

"Chief, I'm telling you, this was not an alligator." "Why Earl? Just because you've hunted and trapped here your whole life?" "It's not that Chief. I'm telling you; the bites just don't match up." "The bites just don't match up? So now you're the authority on gators? What the hell difference does it make anyway? Crocodile or alligator? We will find it and kill "it"." "Chief, we haven't pulled a gator out of this water in ten years. That was a 12-footer. That gator was the county record." "Earl, please get to the point. What are you really trying to say?" "The crocodile that did this is at least 20 feet long."

Chief Hemmingway went back to his house and twisted one up. He took a couple of tokes and turned-on YouTube. The Chief started thinking about what Earl said, then a video caught his eye. "Effects of Weed and Dairy on The Melanin."

(By Da13thsun) https://youtu.be/IPdpcXF3uJo

Then he switched to a lesser-known creator, "Meditation Hidden Wisdom." This guy was a nut. He had all these different types of videos. One video in particular caught the attention of the Chief. The video was a one-minute YouTube short. It was a clip from "The Game of Thrones." Danny was telling her dragon Drogon, to burn the masters. This made the Chief think about what Earl had said. "The crocodile that did this is at least 20 feet long." Chief Hemmingway shuddered at the thought of a real-life dragon being right in the center of Camp StarWess.

The Vibe at Camp StarWess went from hype to somber overnight. The Chief had tried to keep it a secret, but Trish was a stubborn girl. Had the Chief told her to tell as many people as possible, she would have told no one. Be that as it may, Chief Hemingway had asked Trish to tell no one. In respect for the family. Trish had agreed not to say anything. Partly because she didn't know what to say and because she was still in shock. The next day, while Trish was setting in her room waiting for Matts family to arrive; she watched the news. When the news anchor said it had been a 10-to-12-foot alligator who attacked Matt, a chill went down her spine. Trish had been trying her best not to re-think or re-live any of "it". She just blocked all thoughts of the savage attack out of her head. After watching the news, she could not help herself. Trish was now rethinking what happened.

Trish was fast asleep when she heard Matt say, "Whose there." Then she heard a massive SPLASH! When she stood up on the pontoon, she had saw a dragon. Even now as she re-thought what happened fear gripped her, and she let out a yelp. Trish was no herpetologist, but she knew the difference between 10 feet and 20. Trish called the news station and told her story. This changed everything. Pandemonium had struck.

The mayor of Camp StarWess had called Chief Hemingway and told him the cold hard facts. Mayor KeenWits exact words..." There's no way in Hell we are canceling this weekend and refunding all those damn tickets!" This sparked a visceral conversation between the mayor and the chief. "Lives mayor, we're talking about lives!" "No Chief Hemingway we are not talking lives. We're talking about your job! This city runs on this one weekend. Get out there and find that damn Gator!"

"Funny thing about crocodiles is, they can go a long time with out eating." Chief Hemingway then replied, "Earl, are you stupid or just plain old dumb? There are thousands of people on this water right now. At any minute someone could be attacked. But you still must constantly say crocodile this and crocodile that. Please, Earl, just give it a rest!"

BRACKISH WATER, HUMAN WALKER

Earl was right. A croc could go long periods between meals. Lol, if it wanted to. The Salty struck again. This giant saltwater croc, that everyone was told was a gator, struck again! This time the unthinkable happened. Mayor Keenwit was basking in the sun right by the waters edge. The mayor looked at the water and thought to himself, "Damn fools. They believe anything the news tells em. This water aint even safe enough for a dog." The mayor then let out a chuckle. That's the moment everything went horribly wrong. "Go get it girl, go get it!" The mayor screamed "NOOOOO!" Time slowed down as the mayor turned around. What he saw made his stomach sink. Tyler, the mayor's nephew had just thrown Dreems toy football into the lake.

Tyler was stone cold drunk. He had forgotten all about the gator talk. Plus, it was all kinds of boats on the water. Tyler was state champ, and he was celebrating. He just received his acceptance letter from Noter Dame. Even though he was drunk, his arm wasn't. He flung Dreems toy football so hard; the dog couldn't even see were it landed. Dreem, a female Cocker spaniel, had the most beautiful curly black hair. This dog loved to swim but she was a stubborn bitch. No pun intended. Once Dreem hit that water, she would not come back until she got her toy.

Mayor Keenwit screamed NOOOO! It was too late. The Cocker Spaniel had taken off like a bullet. Dreem was swimming like a fish. Tyler was looking at his uncle and laughing. Tyler couldn't understand why the mayor looked so damn sad and serious. "Dreem, Dreem. Treat, Treat. I've got treat, treat." Then the mayor screamed "Dreem!" By this time, Tyler was beside himself. He was rolling on the ground holding his stomach laughing. Laughing so hard tears were coming down his face. Mayor Keenwit stood by the waters edge with his hoarse voice.

The mayor couldn't even scream anymore. Now his calls were a mere whimper. Dreem had not even made it to her toy yet. Then, that's when "it" happened. Sal, the giant saltwater croc, struck again. Sal swam in behind Dreem. Putting himself between the dog and land. Then he started thrashing about to make a spectacle for the people. The mayor saw the splashing of the 20-foot croc and took a step away from the water. He was no longer calling for his dog. He was in shock! Dreem had almost made it to her toy when Sal swallowed her whole. The massive croc didn't even slow down. His huge mouth just opened, and the dog and toy went in. Mayor Keenwit didn't have to give any money back, but he had lost his best friend. This pained him greatly and he declared war on the giant croc.

The weekend was a success. The mayor did not have to refund the tickets and there were no moor fatalities. Sure, Matts family had threatened a civil suit, but he'd pay them off later. Mayor Keenwit had bigger fish to fry. Well, not fish but you get the point. Earl, the game warden and Dr. Yolan met in the mayor's office early Monday morning. Dr. Yolan, the most tenured Herpetologist in the state, was breaking down the dilemma. Dr. Yolan went on to explain, "Lake StarWess is around ten square miles in circumference. There are two smaller streams feeding into Lake StarWess. These two streams bring in saltwater from the ocean. This raises the salinity level of Lake StarWess. Making the water brackish for the most part. This brackish……" The mayor interrupted. "I don't need a science lesson doctor. How do we kill "it"?"

Dr. Yolan shot the mayor a glance and then continued as if he hadn't heard the mayor's comment. "This brackish water has provided enough salinity to sustain this prehistoric beast. We are going to have to disrupt its habitat and force him up one of these two streams." Earl then interjected. "Well, what if we do disrupt his habitat and he doesn't go up either of these streams? What if he decides to swim through the swamp?" "Don't be ridiculous Earl. This time of year, that swamp is only about a foot deep. There is no way in hell this massive croc could traverse five miles through less then a foot of water and mud." "Ok doc let's say he does. What is are recourse?" "Well, that's simple Earl, that's what we have you for. An animal this size would leave a trail so massive even a child could follow. Also, it would take at least 24 hours for him to get to the other body of water. If not longer."

Lake StarWess was a massive body of water. The good thing was that it wasn't that deep. Only 50 feet deep in most places. A croc this size would need sunlight in the morning to regain energy from the cooler night. Two ships were configured with nets. These nets had five-foot square openings in them, to allow other aquatic marine life to pass through. Dr. Yolan devised a device that would directly affect the auditory sensitivity of reptiles. Two ships dredged the lake with nets while thirteen smaller boats blasted sonar. Hunters and trappers from all over the state volunteered for a chance to shoot this present-day dinosaur.

The stage was set. The hunters and trappers surveyed the lakes' edges looking for the croc. Two ships dredged the lake with their massive 100-yard nets. Both streams had patrols eagerly waiting for the croc to try and swim up stream to the ocean. The sonar blasted as the marine life in Lake StarWess went crazy. There was only one problem.

Sal, the saltwater crocodile was no crocodile. Sal was a man masquerading as a crocodile. This giant crocodile was once a man. A man who had made a deal with the devil. Sal had been granted Eternal life and great power. The devil had obliged. Transforming Sal into a giant saltwater crocodile in the process. A saltwater crocodile that could walk on two feet like a man. Sunday night Sal simply walked through the swamp to the next body of water.

BEAUTIFUL MUSIC

_Just as Puma raised the Pendant above his head, the Viscous Ladybug disappeared. She reappeared where Puma had been. Puma narrowly darting away. He bounced off her refrigerator knocking it down. Landing on her bed he let out a ROAR!

Beethoven's 16 Quartet played in Puma's ear. Agent Swims voice buzzed in. "Steady now soldier. Rember the plan is to get her outside, so we can hit her with the heavy artillery." Puma glanced at the door. Then sprung for the opening. The ladybug disappeared then reappeared at the door. The two collided into each other. Puma getting bit in the chest. Then managing to smack one of the ladybugs eyes clean out of the socket. The viscous ladybug Howled! In her most sinister voice, the ladybug spoke. "I'll be in your nightmares hokshila. Then Ms. DoeBoe turned into a beautiful ladybug. She flew right out the window. Puma roared as the Viscous Ladybug escaped beyond his reach.

BEAUTIFUL MUSIC GNIK AND MEARD

Meard- Where you at?

Gnik- Where I'm at?

Meard- Bruh, don't play.

Gnik- Hold on lil momma. Let me go head an chin check dis sh^t right now! Now listen, I'm not gonna be out here eating and beating any otha cat. But if you think you gonna put down on me or boss me around.... GIRL...you done bumped yo got damn head!

Meard- FINE!

NARARATOR- Meard hangs up the phone. Gnik has just picked Meard up, she has just sat down in the car.

Meard- Where are we going!

Gnik- Well got damn.... you still mad?

Meard- why would I have anything to be mad about?

Gnik- Idk. I'm assuming you are. Cuz you aint say hi or try and lean in for a kiss. Do you even know if I smell like another chic or not?

Meard- Pull the car over now! Let me out!

Gnik- Lol. We are going to the facility. And please stop wit da madness. Like...you literally mad, cuz I'm not gonna let you play with my head.

Meard- What you did was way more messed up!

Gnik- How in the hell is that?

Meard- You made a sex clip and sent it to me!
Who does that? What the F^ck kind of time you on
bruh!?

Gnik- N^gga, you were out of the state for months.
Ok, dats cool. Then you pump fake like we are
getting back together. Then you sleep with some
dude you are calling your X. But you met him after
you met me. Dat math don't math. Make it make
sense.

Meard- I'm not going to be able to get that clip out
of my head.

Gnik- That's good. Because you are not going to be
able to beat me. You might have seen a weaker
side of me. Crying about my children or over my
sick mother. But if you think I won't break a bish
down like pound…. you sleep.

Meard- Fine! Why are we going to the facility?

NARARATOR- Gnik doesn't say a word. He calmly
pulls the car over and gets out. Opens up Meards
door and takes her by the hand. He pulls her out
and gives her a big hug and a kiss. They both get
back in the car.

Gnik- Were picking up a subject.

Meard- Wow! So, you lied? You said vacation. This is freaking work sounding to me.

Gnik- "It" is work but it's also a vacation.

Meard- How so?

Gnik- This particular subject needs a vacation.

Meard- Which subject is Et?

Gnik- Girl you know I can't tell you dat.

Meard- Please just tell me. You tell me everything and you know I'm not gonna stop asking. Is "it" Negro?

Meard- YES! Don't ask me sh^t else about this! Just be happy we fixn to be Glamping or whatever da hell you said last week.

NARARATOR- Gnik and Meard arrive at Fort Tashapiathacho. A place with inconceivable beauty in abundance. Two enormous bodies of water and a swamp. Beautiful streams and trees everywhere. With cave systems connecting to the mountains. Five square miles of forest carved in between two mountains. Fort Tasha is a no hunting zone with nature walking freely all around you. Each cabin has 5 acres of land for seclusion. Every cabin comes with 5-star amenities.

Meard- Ok, I take "it" back. This might be nice.

Gnik- Yah think? Just wait to you see inside.

NARARATOR- Gnik and Meard park. Before they go inside Gnik starts the timer to unlock the subject. Once the subject finished his vacation he would return. Gnik would then get an alert.

Gnik- Ok, close your eyes.

Meard- Do I have too?

Gnik- Girl close your eyes.

Gnik- Ok, you can open them now. Tadaah!!!

Meard- WOW! This is mad dope! How much was this?

Gnik- "It" was free. It's free for two days only, perk from the facility.

Meard- Two days? That's not a long-time babe.

Gnik- Girl, you can't sit your hot ass still for two minutes. I'm sure two days will be plenty fine. So, what do you want to do?

Meard- We need to go to the grocery store.

Gnik- Oh wow, you did that on purpose. You knew we had to get groceries before we came all the way up the mountain. Yet, you let me forget.

Meard- So what. I wanted to see the cabin. I've seen the cabin and now I'm in a great mood. But if you keep complaining, I can get bitchey. Do you really want that?

Gnik- No mam. You win. Nough said. Let's go get the groceries.

BEAUTIFUL MUSIC BONDING

Gnik- So who is cooking tonight? Me or you?

Meard- I am silly. What do you want?

NARARATOR- Gniks face lit up like he was a kid in a candy store.

Gnik- Well, in that case, I think I want a....

Meard- Hold up, pause. Just so you know, if you want this big extravagant meal, I'm probably going to be too tired to fool around later.

Gnik- Damn! That's a hell of a decision. Your body or your cooking. I'm going to need a min to think this over.

Meard- Well, if you have to think about "it", I think you should just get neither.

Gnik- That's exactly why we make such a great team. Because I don't let you do the thinking for me. Now, let me see. I think I want some black bean burgers. Oh, and some of your homemade banana vegan ice cream too. And then....

NARARATOR- Meard is just looking at Gnik with her eye browns contorted. Trying to figure out if Gnik is serious or not.

Gnik- And then we can go to that little adult store that we saw on the way down the mountain. You can get whatever you like. Then later, I can chit chat dat chinchilla. Give you that feeling that you like so much. You know the one. The one where you can't feel your legs?

Meard- There is a word to describe you but I just cant think of it now. How many other girls have you used that line on?

Gnik- Don't matter. You like it. When I said, "Chit chat dat chinchilla", you started smiling. So, stop the shenanigans.

NARARATOR- The two life partners leave the grocery store and head to Tempest X to pick up some toys. They pick up some toys and head back to the cabin. After they eat, they go on a long walk around the property. They take a shower. Party like rock stars and then the pillow talk starts.

Meard- This is the best night ever. It's making me a little sad though.

Gnik- Why?

Meard- When we leave here, we have to go back to the grind. This place is so magical. Why do people have to work?

Gnik- That's simple. People are lazy and idle hands are the devil's workshop. The people that can control their passions and impulses can use their mind to generate currency. When you get to a certain level spiritually, you will never work a day in your life again.

Meard- How is that?

Gnik- When you connect to your higher self, you have a higher inner standing of yourself. When you truly know who you are, you can then maximize the gifts the CREATORS gave you.

Meard- What gifts? Like, gifts don't pay bills. Money does.

Gnik- Well what about your writing? I think it's dope!

Meard- Yeah but you said I would probably have to sell my soul to be a bestselling author.

Gnik- That's not exactly what I said. I said If you want to be famous in this world, you must give up the universe.

Meard- I don't understand. What's the difference?

Gnik- You can manifest yourself to be very fortunate. In this way you can have fortune without the fame.

Meard- Well, how do I manifest myself to fortune?

Gnik-Sacrifice! Everything comes with a price.

Meard- Are you saying what I think you're saying?

Gnik- There are many forms of sacrifice. Some chose humans and animals. The people who practice human and animal sacrifices are looking outside of themselves for validation. They are operating on a very low frequency/vibration. Yes, the magic they wield is powerful, but it comes with a price. To gain world renown on this planet you must give up the universe. Once you sign a soul contract you can never leave this planet. Because you will be agreeing to turn a blind eye to the plight of the human race.

Meard- Dats deep. But what are some other types of sacrifices?

Gnik- The most powerful sacrifice I practice is fasting. Everyone has a destructive habit that they do, even though they know it's bad for them. If you abstain and fast during prayer and or deep meditation, your manifestations come true rapidly and abundantly.

Meard- So what do you think about...

Gnik- Girl stop stalling. Is you ready for round two or not?

Meard- Why not, we're already naked anyways.

BEAUTIFUL MUSIC ANCIENT

Powerful footsteps can be heard trampling through the forest. The birds chirping stops. The owls aren't hooting. Something is amiss. The powerful thud of feet creeping through the forest is getting louder. Puma is twenty-five feet in the air, sleeping on a tree limb. When Puma awakes, he's instantly alert. He's got a weird feeling. Puma thinks to himself, "What is this feeling?" The footsteps grow louder and get closer. Pumas' spine tingles and the fur on the back of his neck is raised. "Just what the hell is this feeling?"

Then Et happens! Pumas' cat eyes spot a walking monster, a dragon. The enormous monster walks right under the limb he is perched on. Puma realizes what this feeling is. ITS FEAR! The massive monstrosity walks right by Puma. Puma is thinking to himself, "This is abnormal. Outside of nature. I've got to do something!" Frozen in fear, Puma can't move a muscle. The sheer size and girth of this monster has frightened Puma. The Enormous monster continued walking through the forest. Unimpeded by the one thing that could stop him.

 An hour passed before Puma slinked down the tree. The scent left by this monster was unmistakable. Puma did not have his earpiece in. He was supposed to be on vacation, whatever the hell that was. Puma decided he would track the creature. Whenever the creature decided to take cover, Puma would report back to Agent Swim. After about four miles, the scent lead Puma to the kennel he was released from. Puma darted into the cabin.

Inside the cabin was a scene likened to a battlefield. To the untrained eye "it" would look like a war had taken place. That's not what happened at all. The monster had crashed in through the bedroom wall. Taken Gnik and Meard by surprise. Still, the two highly trained agents had let off over a hundred rounds. The two agents had Glocks with silencers on them. No big guns. They were not hunters, they were guards. Puma let out a loud ROAR! All that was left was blood. The monster had not only killed them, but he had also eaten the remains.

Pumas' fear was replaced with rage. Now he was not tracking the monster, he was in hot pursuit. Bouncing and darting through the wooded area, Puma let out a mighty Roar! His fear had cost him dearly. Meard and Gnik were his friends. Although they didn't have much direct contact with each other. Gnik had picked out this beautiful place and told Puma he needed a vacation. Meard had always called Puma negro because of his black fur. Meard had lost her life because of his fear. The fear left. There was only rage.

Puma finally tracked him down. He roared as the massive monster slowed down and then turned to face him. Sal let out a chuckle. Puma and Sal were eye to eye, merely 13 feet apart. Sal continued to laugh and then said. "Coward! I smelt your scent hours ago. I was so close to you I could taste you. Coward! You sat somewhere perfectly still. I bet you didn't even move a whisker." Puma roared massively. Sal, the Saltwater crocodile continued to laugh. "No matter. I love eating cat for dessert anyways!" The massive croc now stood up on his back legs and continued to laugh. "You tracked me for a reason. Now lets get on with "it"!"

Puma looked up at the massive croc standing nearly 20 feet tall. He calculated in his head that he could easily jump up to the crocs head. But then what? Puma roared again and flexed his claws out. He thought to himself, "I could never win this fight. Even still I will surely die. This will be a good death. I would rather die on my claws than live with the shame of fear." Puma took a couple of bounces and then shot straight up into the air. Right before he made contact with Sal, his pendant was removed. Puma was now the boy. Time stood still as my ancient ancestor appeared to him. Mary Molly aka Tashapiathacho called out to Puma. "Keysari." Puma was in a daze. He did not respond.

"Keysari." Puma recognized the name, but it was not his own. He had heard that name before. Et was familiar to him but why? This time in a more intimate and loving tone, the ancient ancestor spoke again. "Keysari." Puma now realized why he knew that name. Keysari was the name of The Boy and The Pendant. Keysari was Puma in human form. Puma answered. "Yes." "Keysari, why do you sacrifice your life in this manner? This is a battle that you can not physically win?"

The boy replied, "I will win. I must!" "Yes, you have lost many and suffered greatly in your lifetime. Your time is Now! The wrongs will be righted. I will see to that. My blood is your blood. Our blood is one. Your present actions will bring your life force to an end. Et is not your time to die. I will grant you the power of a Siberian Tiger. The largest of all living big cats. This monster will die, but not today." Puma woke up on a tree limb with

Beethoven's 25th quartet Moonlight Sonata, playing in his mind.

THE STORY OF A MAN

Jhonny called out to the children. "ROAD TRIP!" Three sets of feet slammed down on the mahogany wood floors. The boys were up and ready. Jhonny and his wife April were taking the boys to the country. This was no pitter patter of feet. This was a stampede! The boys raced each other to the steps. Each one wanting to make "it" to their dad first, so they could ask where the road trip was to. Jhonny Jr., the oldest, was first down the steps. The twins, Jason and Jimmy, were fast on his trail. Even though Jhonny Jr. was 13, he had his hands full with the twins. The twins worked together instinctively as one.

Just as Jhonny Jr. was in full sprint, the heavens collapsed. Jason, the oldest of the twins, dropped his bedspread and pillows down on Jhonny Jr. Jhonny Jr. tripped and fell with the bedspread over his head and the pillows breaking his fall. Jimmy jumped over his older brother and shouted, "Lil

Jit!" Jhonny Jr. being seven years older than his brothers, always called them lil jits. Jason shouted down from the banister to his older brother, "Gang, Gang, Twin Gang!" Jhonny Jr. laid on the floor with his arms crossed. He wasn't even angry. He loved his little brothers. Jhonny Jr. considered himself a knife and his brothers were the sharpening stone.

  Jimmy slid up to his father and shouted, "Twin Gang!" Jhonny Sr. and his son did the patented Salvator handshake. "Where are we going dad?" "You and your brother go get the bedspread off JJ. Help him up and then I'll tell y'all together. I'm all for Twin Gang and big brother competition but y'all cheated and he could have gotten hurt." Jason, now shooting into the kitchen said, "Did we get him? Where are we going?" Jimmy replied to Jason, "Dad said we cheated. We need to help JJ up." The twins helped their brother up and the three of them walked into the kitchen together.

  "April, get off that darn phone. Lets tell the boys where we are going." April hung the phone up and walked into the kitchen. Jhonny Sr. began to speak. "Ok boys, we are going to Trim Tree Creek!"

Jhonny Jr. repeated what his dad said, "Trim Tree Creek?" The twins began to shout, "TRIM TREE CREEK, TRIM TREE CREEK!" Jhonny Jr. had a puzzled look on his face. Then he said, "Dad, where is Trim Tree Creek?" Jhonny Sr. just smiled at his son and said. "Go get ready." The twins continued chanting, "Trim Tree Creek, Trim Tree Creek!"

The twins were still chanting Trim Tree Creek when they pulled up at their father's office. JJ, the oldest of the boys said, "Dad, why are we at your office?" Jhonny Sr. replied to his son, "This is not an office. This is a way of life. Today, I teach you boys that way of life." The twins stopped chanting and Jason said, "Hey, wait a minute. What's going on?" April looked at her husband and said, "Yeah dad, what's going on?" Jhonny Sr. thought to himself, "Got damn that women is a traitor. She knows good and got damn well what's going on. We talked about this last night. Now she is playing dumb so the boys will just be mad at me for trying to teach them the family business."

"Today is the day I teach you young men the family business. There is a creek in the back of the office. I'm going to teach you how to trim trees." JJ became angry because he had figured out what the twins had not. JJ spurted out, "You lied to us dad?" "No son, I did not. I told you we are going to Trim Tree Creek. There is a creek as I've just told you and we will be trimming trees." Now the twins had figured out what was going on. Jimmy shouted out to his father, "This sucks dad!" Jason looked at his mother. His mother just looked away. April knew the boys needed to be taught responsibility. Tricking "her boys" like this angered her. She hated the way Jhonny manipulated them like this.

  All and all, et was a pretty productive day. The twins basically played in the creek all day. Jhonny and JJ had trimmed the trees and actually had a good time. April stayed on the phone in between playing with the twins. JJ asked his father a lot of questions. The boy had really taken an interest in the family business. Not so much the work aspect but the numbers. "How much did you say you make a week dad?" Jhonny Sr. replied, "Well son, I make about 3 k a week." "And how much did you say I'll be making when I start working with you?" "I don't know JJ. Depends on how good you are. If you start helping now and training, by the time you're 16, I'll give you 16 an hour." "That doesn't sound like much. Is that a lot dad?" "Sure it is JJ, sure it is."

JJ helped his father carry the twins in. He wanted to talk to his father more about the numbers. JJ loved numbers. "Ok dad, so you said you gross 3 k a week, right? What happens after that?" "Well Junior, after that is a thing called Net. I must pay workers compensation, insurance and taxes." "Well then, how much is left after that?" "Around 2 k." "Ok, ok. And how much is mom's net?" "Well, your mom makes a little bit more than me. She makes around 2300 a week net." "Wow, mom makes 1200 more than you a month! Twelve-hundred dollars more a month doesn't sound like a little bit dad. And if its only a little bit more, can I have 1200 dollars for my birthday then?"

THE STORY OF A MAN, FATHERSHIP

"It" was the 9th of April, but "it" felt like summer. The boys were sleep and Jhonny Sr. had just awoken from a cat nap. The four of them had played touch football from breakfast to lunch. Every Sunday for two years this had been a tradition. Normally Jhonny Sr. and the boys slept for an hour or two. Today Jhonny Sr. woke up after only about fifteen minutes. He wasn't comfortable. His back was hurting, and he needed to stretch. Jhonny Sr. got up and decided to go check on his wife. And again, she was on the phone.

As Jhonny Sr. came down the steps, he heard his wife talking. Not wanting to ease drop on her conversation, he decided to announce himself. "April! Who you talking to ma?" April yelped. He had caught her by surprise. She just hung the phone up and said, "Jen." "Jen", Jhonny thought to himself. "That doesn't make sense. Jen went to the south pole to see the land beyond the ice wall." Even though Jen was his wife's friend, Jhonny knew more about her comings and goings then his wife did. Summer came early this year. It was April but everything was growing rapidly. Jen was Johnny's' customer. Jen had given Jhonny explicit instructions for her fruit trees. She said she would be gone for several months and would have no cell service.

Jhonny decided to dig a little deeper. Jen had given him all these instructions just two days ago. There was no way she was back already. There were only two possible scenarios. Jen had not gone on her trip or April was lying. "So, what did she say ma? Is she really enjoying her trip to the Bahamas?" April stiffened a little bit, her heart beating out of her chest. "Yeah babe, she loves it." Jhonny felt a ping in his heart. That ping then grew to an ache. She had lied. April had lied. She wasn't talking to Jen. Then who the hell was she talking to?

Jhonny decided to go Debo. He would ask her for her phone. If she said no, he would take her phone. April had never lied before. Why now? "Aye babe, funny thing is, Jen is not in the Bahamas. She is at the south pole. Did you forget she has been my customer for the last three months?" Now the beating in April's heart was a pounding action. Her stomach began to knot up. This was "it". The thing she had feared all this time. Pandoras Box was now open! April did not reply. She just turned around to face her husband. Soon as they made eye contact, Jhonny knew.

"How long?" The tears began to roll down April's face. She was not sad she had gotten caught. No, these were tears of relief. The lie was over. It was truth telling time. Jhonny Sr. called out to his wife again. "How long?" She could lie no more. The truth cut like a Yoda light saber. "Thirteen years!" 'Wtf! So, you started an affair right after Junior was born?" "JJ is turning 14 next week. That well make "it" 14 years." There, she had said it. Hopefully her husband had caught the truth of the matter. Now tears started rolling down Johnny's face. "So, Junior isn't Junior?" April did love Jhonny and it hurt her to hurt him. No matter, she had to speak her truth. "Jhonny, I begged you not to name him after you. You would not listen."

And there "it" was, The cold hard facts. Jhonny had more questions, but he feared the answers. Tears rolled down his face moor rapidly now. He went upstairs and looked at his boys. Wondering if at least the twins were his. But too scared to ask April. Jhonny went to the master bedroom and began to pack his things. He hurt so bad, he wanted to fall on the floor in a fetal position and cry his heart out. There was still one question he wanted an answer to.

Jhonny went downstairs with his bags packed and sat them down. He walked into the kitchen. His wife was sitting at the table with a blank stare on her face. Jhonny summoned up the strength for a chuckle. He looked at his wife and said, "Thanks ma, I mean for the honesty. I just have one question. I don't even want to know why. I just need to know the who. Who is he?" April was in shock. She thought she would feel better after telling him her secret. Now all she felt was pain for the boys. For all of them. "April! I said, who is He!" April blinked a couple of times and then kept up with the honesty. "Vegas!"

Now everything all made sense. Jhonny and April got married 20 years ago. They had tried to have children for several years. Then all of the sudden, April had gotten a new job and then pregnant soon after. April had begged Jhonny for five years to come to the fertility doctor with her. Jhonny never went with her because he did not want children. It was only after Jhonny Jr. was born, that Jhonny now loved children.

Jhonny repeated what his wife said. "VEGAS!" You mean your boss? Your boss Vegas?" April had a stoic look on her face. She simply replied, "Yes Jhonny. Vegas my boss." Now something snapped in Jhonny. The tears dried up and the pain in his gut was gone. Vegas and his wife Karen had always been extra, they had always done the most. Throughout her job at the accounting agency, April had kept receiving raises and vacation days. Any time they would go on vacation, Vegas and Karen would always watch the boys for them.

Now the true plot had unfolded. They had played Jhonny like a loose fiddle on Sunday at the poor folk's blues bar. Jhonny had a smirk on his face as he looked at his wife. He turned, walked right past his bags and left the house.

THE STORY OF A MANS SOUL

The last two months had gone horribly for Johnny, but he didn't seem to care. Jhonny had moved out of the house and left it to April and the boys. One day, when he came by to visit, the door was unlocked, and all the furniture was gone. The only thing in the house was a note on the back of the door. The note read, "Sorry Jhonny, I just can't anymore. The boys and I are moving upstate." Jhonny read the letter, crumpled it up and calmly walked out of the house. Four weeks after that, Jhonny had not heard from April or the boys. He didn't even know where they were.

Exactly four weeks after April and the boys moved, Jhonny got a letter in the mail. It was DNA results. He calmly opened the results. He read them and found out that the twins were not his either. Jhonny crumpled up the letter, smiled and then turned the tv on. He finished watching his favorite show and then went upstairs to pack his toolbox. Only two words were running through Jhonny's head "Road Trip!"

Just as Jhonny arrived at his motel, he was struck with an epiphany. His favorite movie was "Officer and Gentlemen." Jhonny walked into the little motel with a reenactment on his mind. He paid for his room and then said, "Watch this!" Jhonny took his wedding ring off and then swallowed it. The motel clerk said, "Here is your key weirdo." Jhonny just smiled and said, "You don't even know the half bro." He took the key from the clerk and started singing. "Love lift us up where we belong!" While Jhonny was exiting the motel lobby, the clerk repeated the same word again, "Weirdo!?

Jhonny was ready to make his deal with the devil. Good or bad. Didn't matter, he was willing to live with "IT". He walked out of his motel room with toolbox in hand and a great smile on his face. Jhonny had recently liquidated his assets and bought a new car. He had a bright red Charger RT with the Hemi engine. He thought to himself, "This damn thing is loud." Jhonny hopped in the car and pushed the start button. The Hemi engine began to purr like a tiger who was about to be let out of a cage. He put her in reverse, then in drive and tore off. All you heard was the screeching of tires as the Charger got sideways.

Jhonny turned on his music. His favorite song was locked into repeat. It was Sade, "Hang on to your love". Sade had just said his favorite line, "Why are you walking away? Why do you play these games?" When he looked in the rearview mirror, Jhonny saw smoke and black tire marks. He sped up the mountain with nerves of steel. He almost hoped he would kill himself, although that was not his mission. He was speeding up the mountain doing 100 miles an hour. The only way he could keep her on the road was to ride in the middle of the two-lane road.

If at any moment a car was coming down the mountain, there would be a horrible crash. "It" was inevitable, something would have to give. Either he would wreck, the other car would wreck, or they both would. Either way, the stakes were feisty and high. Jhonny approached the top of the mountain with his hemi roaring. There was only one driveway and one house. He revved up the engine a bit and pulled in the driveway. Jhonny got out of the car and grabbed his toolbox. He put on his shades and headed toward the front door. He rung the bell. With his dark glasses and palm-tree shirt on, no one even recognized him. The door was opened. When the child spoke to Jhonny, he patted him on the head and walked right by him.

The child said, "Hey Mr., I didn't say enter! Dad!" The child was hollering for his father while Jhonny walked into the kitchen. He said hello to the lady. The lady dropped her glass on the floor. The glass shattered. Jhonny opened up his toolbox and took out his gun. The lady just froze, unable to move. Jhonny took off his glasses and said, "Hi April." He let two shots go and then said, "By April."

Vegas had broken up with his wife Karen. He had come clean and told her the truth. Vegas, April and the boys had moved upstate to a house on a mountain. They were going to have their happily ever after; or so they thought. What they didn't count on was Jhonny and Karen wanting revenge. Karen felt just as much pain as Jhonny had, if not more. Karen found out where Jhonny lived and had come to his apartment one night. She had rung his bell with a big bottle of Hennessy in her arms. When Jhonny answered the door, Karen said, "I know where they're at. But you must promise me that you will kill them both!" Then she walked into Johnny's apartment.

Vegas heard the shots. He grabbed his gun and ran down the steps. He shoved the boys into the living room closet. Vegas cocked his snub nose 357 and was ready to get active. He walked into the room and was bewildered. April had blood everywhere and a man was lying on the floor with blood on his face. Vegas got a couple of feet closer with his gun pointed right at the intruder. It looked like the man had shot April and then taken his own life. Vegas took a peak over at April and then fell to the ground. He had not heard the shot that burst his brain open. Jhonny was playing possum. Soon as Vegas looked over at April, Jhonny shot him dead.

A year later, Jhonny Salvator was found guilty of murder in the first-degree times two. During his trial Karen had come to see him for the entire year. They had fallen in love. Jhonny had greatly miscalculated. His favorite show was CSI. He figured he would only get 20 to 25 years since he did not premeditate the murders. Although, he did not premeditate his wife's murder, the jury found that he had premeditated April's lover Vegas's murder. Instead of getting 20 to 25 years, Jhonny was getting the chair. When sentencing was read Karen screamed at the top of her lungs. She started hollering at the judge, "Do you know what they did to us!? They did this to themselves!!!" Karen had to be restrained and Jhonny was taken back to his holding cell.

Jhonny sat in his holding cell thinking to himself. Then he said out loud, "I'd give anything to be out of this cell and live a life with Karen." An old lady's creaky witch voice could be heard saying, "Anything?" Jhonny thought his mind was playing tricks on him. An old lady had just disappeared on one side of his holding cell. Then reappeared inside his holding cell. "Did you say anything boy?" Jhonny blinked a couple times and started smacking himself in the face and saying, "You're not real, You're not real!" When he opened his eyes again, he screamed. The woman had turned into a monster.

"I've come to collect your soul boy. You can die now, or you can barter with your soul." Jhonny screamed again and then urinated on himself. The

Viscous Lady bug he saw before him, had him terrified. He sputtered out a word. "B-b-b-arter?" The old lady began to speak. "Yes, you foolish boy. I have the power to grant you immortality and power beyond your wildest dreams." "And--- all.... You want is my soul?" The lady answered, "Yes, among other things, but for now let's start with your soul. Where you're going you wouldn't need Et anyways." Jhonny had nothing to lose. He said "OK!" The old lady then said. "It" is done!"

Jhonny had great pain in his stomach, and he fell to the ground. The old lady began to laugh in an Erie gleeful way. Jhonny began to thrash about on the ground as his body began to swell and grow. Yelling and screaming, Jhonny tore at his flesh. The pain was unbearable, and the witch just kept watching and laughing.

Forty-two seconds later, the transformation had been completed. Jhonny could barely fit in his cell. Jhonny now had a monstrous voice. He called out to old lady DoeBoe, "What HAVE YOU DONE TO ME!" To which the old lady tersely replied, "Order of the Hidden!" The massive monster began to thrash around and burst out of his cell. The monster was running on two feet. Just as Sal, the saltwater croc approached LakeWess, he said two words, "Wendell Eternal!"

THANK YOU FOR YOUR TIME